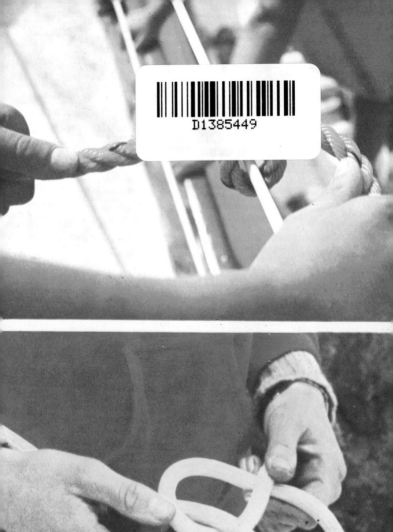

This is a practical book about making and using knots. The knots described here have been chosen for their usefulness, and ease of making. In most cases they could almost be said to have 'chosen themselves' because many of them have been used for a very long time, and turn up on home-made objects in many parts of the world. They were well-established by the time they were described in the seamen's manuals of the early 19th century.

We usually think of sailors in connection with knot-tying, but people in most occupations need to tie a knot at some time or other, and you find recognisable knots turning up on old farm implements, and on hunting and fishing gear world-wide. Keep your eyes open next time you go on holiday, or read an old book, or visit a museum. If it worked for someone else, it may be of use to you!

ACKNOWLEDGMENTS

The publishers wish to thank Bridon Fibres and Plastics Ltd for permission to reproduce the photograph of a rope walk on pages 6–7, Mr Peter Oates for the photograph on page 45, and Mr Walt Unsworth of *Climber and Rambler* magazine for the photograph on pages 22–23, also the bottom photograph on page 1.

Knots

by RONALD A. L. HINTON
illustrations by ERIC WINTER and FRANK HUMPHRIS
photographs by JOHN MOYES and TIM CLARK

Ladybird Books Ltd Loughborough 1977

Ropes in history

Descriptions of knots in this book generally refer to 'rope', but of course you can tie knots in all sorts of string, cord and thread, or in strips of leather and cloth, or lengths of wire. Early Stone Age Man learned to plait simple ropes of hide, and by the time the Ancient Egyptians were building their great stone monuments thousands of years ago, they had learned to make massive ropes with which sweating teams of slaves dragged the enormous blocks of stone to the building sites.

By 200 BC man had learned to twist ropes of vegetable fibres, and hemp was the most popular source of rope fibre from that time until the 19th century, when manila and other substitutes came into use as the Philippines and other new trading areas were opened up.

These vegetable fibres are very short, and to be of use they have to be carefully spun together into yarn, which is then twisted together into the strands from which the rope is to be made.

Building a Pyramid

The making of rope

The place where the final rope is made has to be very long, and is called a *Rope Walk*, a detail of which is shown below. A gear-system gives the same twist to each of the three strands which are led through holes in the block, and then lie together evenly. The made-up rope is drawn off and allowed to turn freely. In fact the three strands lay themselves together in a direction opposite to the twist given to them by the gear-wheels. The twist of most ordinary ropes runs in an anti-clockwise direction, looking at an end.

Man-made fibres are now widely used in rope making. They are rot-proof and can be very strong. The fibres themselves can be made very long, in the first place. You may even have seen single-strand nylon fishing-line which is *extruded* (squeezed out) in one long strand, at first rather like syrup. This hardens to a strong, smooth thread.

Nylon ropes first appeared in the nineteen-fifties, and Terylene and polypropylene more recently. They are often braided into a multi-strand cord, and brightly-coloured ropes of 'polyprop' are now a familiar sight.

Handling of ropes

The type of three-stranded, twisted rope made in the rope walk on the previous page is known as a *hawser-laid* rope. The direction of twist of the rope does affect its use, because it can cause unwelcome twisting and kinking, and perhaps danger to the user, if not handled properly. The common type of rope, with the direction of twist shown here, should be coiled in a clockwise direction. This eliminates kinks in the rope, which always tends to twist when it is bent.

Notice however that when you coil spare rope at the end of a line which is in use, you must begin your coil where the slack rope first reaches the ground. Then any twist caused by coiling is run off the end of the rope. If you begin your coil at the end of the rope, you end up with a series of kinks in the standing part and they are difficult to get rid of.

Provided that the ends of a rope are held together, it will not unravel, because the twisting of its component yarns during manufacture holds it together in a compact and useful shape. However, if you use a rope repeatedly you will soon find that the ends begin to fray and open up, if no action is taken to stop this happening. You get this problem with braided nylon ropes and cords just as much as with an ordinary hawser-laid rope.

Some modern ropes are sold with a rubber band at each end, or if they are made of nylon or polypropylene they are singed to make the ends melt slightly and stick together. The traditional method of stopping fraying is by *whipping* the end of the rope with fine twine. If you have a rope of any size which you want to use often, it is well worth doing this for yourself. One form of whipping is found on pages 46-47, but we will describe the simpler *West-Country Whipping* after describing the *Reef Knot* with which it is finished.

Reef knot

The Reef Knot is one of the most popular and useful knots for joining two ends of rope together over a parcel or reefed sail. The classical way of tying it is shown below.

Take an end of rope in each hand and lay the left-hand end over the right. Then using your right hand, take the end from the left down behind the other rope and up to the front again. Point the ends inwards again, this time the one in your right hand over the other one, down behind it and up to the front through the loop which has now been formed.

The finished knot looks like the one in our illustration, and consists of two interlocking loops.

This is a very neat and flat knot, and is useful for tying the ends of a bandage, or wherever you need a flat, tidy join. It is also very secure as long as the two pieces of rope are of similar thickness. Notice that each rope end lies on the same side of the loop as the rope to which it belongs. If they are on opposite sides you have a *Granny Knot*, which is ugly and unsafe.

Granny Knot

When you have mastered the traditional way of tying the Reef Knot, take one of the ends, and the rope to which it belongs, and pull them apart as in the diagram, so that this rope is stretched straight between your hands.

Reef Knot

Lark's Head

The other rope will now be hanging on this stretched rope in the form of a double looped hitch called a *Lark's Head*, sometimes used to attach a rope to a ring or a bar. The Lark's Head can be slid off the rope to dismantle the knot. Another way of making a Reef Knot: make a Lark's Head, slide a straight rope end through it, and 'upset' the Lark's Head by opening up the loop with your thumb. It will then only need tightening. With this method you can pull the straight end through the Lark's Head to tighten your ropes before finishing the knot.

The two *ends* in a Reef Knot of course lie on the same side of the knot. Some sailors however would close their kit-bags with a *Thief Knot*, where the ends lie on opposite sides of the knot. Anyone tampering with the kit-bag

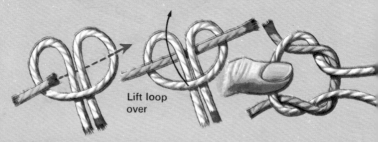

Lift loop over

would re-tie it with a normal Reef Knot, and the difference would quickly be spotted. This Thief Knot can only be tied by the Lark's Head method.

Reef Knot

Thief Knot

West-Country whipping

The *West-Country Whipping* mentioned earlier is best done with a ready-cut piece of twine.

Starting about three rope-thicknesses from the end of the rope, place the middle of your twine across the back of your rope as in 1. Bring both ends (in opposite directions) round to the front of the rope and cross them with a half-hitch as in 2.

1

2

Take the ends round to the back again and tie another half-hitch, then back to the front for the same again, as in 3, and so on, nearly to the end of the rope. Finish the whipping with a full Reef Knot, as in 4.

3

To make the West-Country Whipping as neat and secure as possible you need to make the half-hitches tight, and as even and level as possible. Don't go too close to the end of the rope, or the last turn, with its Reef Knot, may slip off.

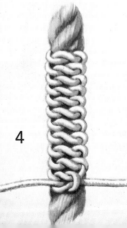

4

Overhand knot and a Quipu

Although most people have heard of the Reef Knot, they would tie this knot if you said, 'Tie a knot in this string':

The proper name of this knot is the *Overhand Knot*, and it has its uses for stopping things sliding off a string. No doubt you have used it for a conker, and your mother would use it at the end of her sewing-thread. It has probably been in use for thousands of years. We know that the Incas in Peru used it to record things which they were counting, on a device called a *Quipu*.

This was made up of a number of strings hanging from a short main cord. Groups of knots were made on these hanging strings, so that they formed rows across the Quipu. The row next to the main cord showed Thousands, below this Hundreds, then Tens, and right at the bottom of the strings were the 'Ones'. Sometimes the 'Ones' were shown by an Overhand Knot with many turns (six turns would mean the number 'Six'). Otherwise knots were grouped closely together to show each number. Each string showed one particular 'count'.

They are believed to have used coloured cords to show what had been counted, such as red for warriors ready for war, green for those killed in battle, and so on.

Some Peruvian shepherds still use a Quipu in counting their flocks.

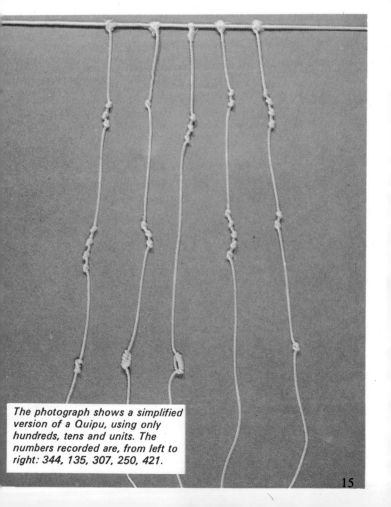

The photograph shows a simplified version of a Quipu, using only hundreds, tens and units. The numbers recorded are, from left to right: 344, 135, 307, 250, 421.

Speed in 'Knots'

Another piece of equipment marked out by a series of knots was the *Log Line* used by sailors to measure the speed of their ship. The *Log* was a wooden board, or metal gadget designed to have sufficient 'drag' in the water to hold the end of the line steady in the water while the ship forged ahead, pulling out the line. The man using it counted the number of knots passing overboard in a given time (originally half-a-minute).

The knots were spaced so that one 'knot' represented a speed of one nautical mile-per-hour. So this is now referred to as a speed of 'one knot'.

A line with knots one fathom (six feet) apart was used as a 'sounding line' to measure the depth of water beneath the ship. A lead weight on its end took it to the bottom, and once again the user counted the knots to reckon up the depth in fathoms.

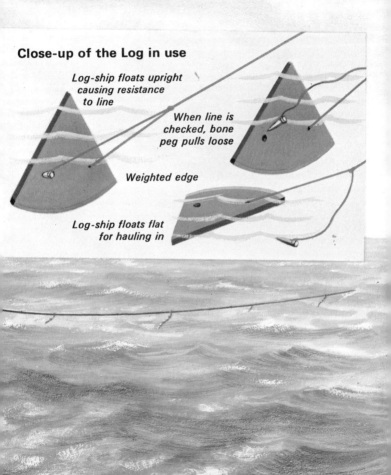

Close-up of the Log in use

Log-ship floats upright causing resistance to line

When line is checked, bone peg pulls loose

Weighted edge

Log-ship floats flat for hauling in

Fishermen's knots

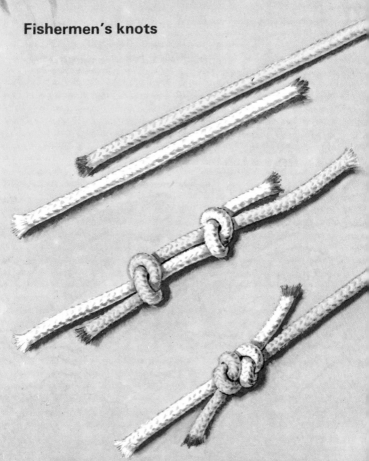

The Overhand Knot is also used to make the *Fisherman's Knot*, which is used to join sections of line together. The two ends to be joined are laid parallel, but pointing in opposite directions. Each end then makes an Overhand Knot around the line lying alongside, and the two knots are pulled together.

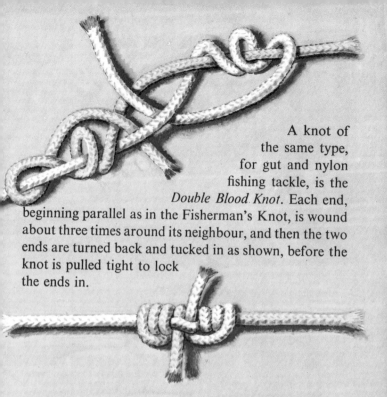

A knot of
the same type,
for gut and nylon
fishing tackle, is the
Double Blood Knot. Each end,
beginning parallel as in the Fisherman's Knot, is wound
about three times around its neighbour, and then the two
ends are turned back and tucked in as shown, before the
knot is pulled tight to lock
the ends in.

A useful fixed loop can be made at the end of a rope
by bending it back into a loop, or *bight* as the sailors
call it, and then tying a *Double Overhand Knot* in the
double thickness of rope as shown. We will find on page
26 that such a loop makes a good start for a really tight
tie round a bundle or parcel. Tied with two *ends* instead
of a bight, it can be used for joining string (but not
very neatly!)

Figure-of-Eight knot

An even more useful overhand knot is the *Figure-of-Eight Knot*. For this knot you must make a loop with the sides crossing over, as in the picture. Hold the crossover with the right finger and thumb. Take the loop in the left-hand finger and thumb, and twist it over until it is upside-down. Then pull the right-hand rope-end up through the loop, and pull tight. This knot is a useful 'stopper-knot' to stop things coming off the rope, or to stop the rope slipping through a hole. Since it holds well on nylon or catgut, it is chosen by the violinist to attach a gut string to the tail-piece of his instrument.

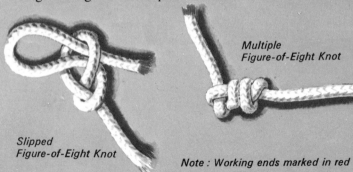

*Multiple
Figure-of-Eight Knot*

*Slipped
Figure-of-Eight Knot*

Note : Working ends marked in red

20

If you need a thicker stopper either tuck in a small bight at the end to make a *Slipped Figure-of-Eight* or twist the loop over several times before bringing the end through, and tighten the knot by drawing it through your fingers. The one in the picture was made by turning the loop over five times, but it needed quite a lot of joggling to make it neat.

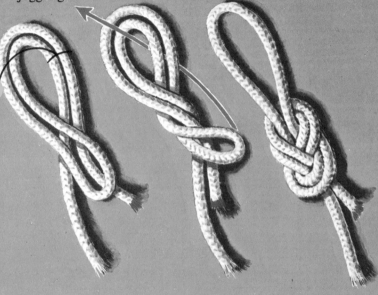

The ordinary Figure-of-Eight knot made with a doubled-back piece of rope makes a loop which is very firm and safe. Take the loop made by doubling the rope, and cross it over for the beginning of a Figure-of-Eight as in the picture. Hold it in your right hand and by actually putting your left index finger in the double loop from behind, turn it over once, and bring the single loop in from the back and through the double loop.

Double Figure-of-Eight knot

On a small scale, this Double Figure-of-Eight, some-times called the *Flemish Eye Knot*, can be used to make a loop at the end of a fishing cast for the attachment of the line. On a larger scale, it is one of the knots recom-mended for climbers to attach their safety-ropes to waist belts, slings, etc. Besides being made at the end of a rope (with an extra Overhand Knot for safety with nylon ropes), it can also be made in mid-rope as in the attachment of the climber's *belay* in the picture. In this position a loop of rope is threaded through a carabiner on the waist sling, and doubled back on itself to make the figure-of-eight. The end loop, perhaps thirty centimetres long, hangs free, so that the knot is safe, but easily undone. This could be used for direct attachment of a safety rope to the body (alternatively a *Bowline* could be used.)

The Bowline

This is another old sailor's knot. It can easily be tied around your waist. To tie a Bowline, hold the rope in both hands and lay it back in a small round loop, 1. Bring up the end of the rope from behind, through the loop, round the standing part of the rope and back down through the loop again, 2 and 3. Perhaps you will remember it by the old scouts' saying about the rabbit

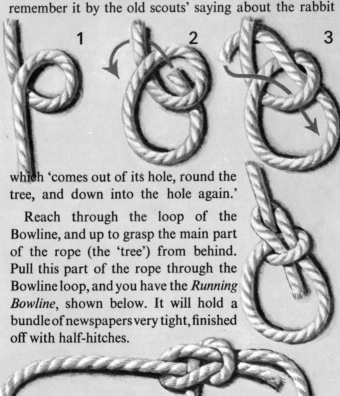

which 'comes out of its hole, round the tree, and down into the hole again.'

Reach through the loop of the Bowline, and up to grasp the main part of the rope (the 'tree') from behind. Pull this part of the rope through the Bowline loop, and you have the *Running Bowline*, shown below. It will hold a bundle of newspapers very tight, finished off with half-hitches.

Running Bowline

Another interesting version of the Bowline is the *Bowline-on-a-Bight* with its two loops. The rope is first doubled back to form the bight which is then laid back to make a *double* 'rabbit-hole' loop. The end loop or bight is brought through this from behind as in the ordinary Bowline, but then, instead of 'going round the tree', this bight is opened out and turned back on itself

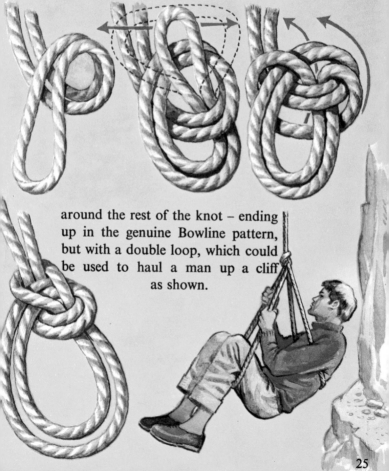

around the rest of the knot – ending up in the genuine Bowline pattern, but with a double loop, which could be used to haul a man up a cliff as shown.

Knots for parcels

For everyday parcels going through the post a tie based on the Running Bowline or the *Running Overhand Loop* (see page 19) is best.

Make a Bowline, or the Double Overhand Knot described on page 19. Holding this loop at the front of the parcel, pass the string round the back and bring it back up through the loop. Then take the string at right-angles to the first tie, round the parcel again and back to the first knot. There take it through the loop and make two half-hitches round the string on the other side.

Some people take a half-hitch or an Overhand Knot around the crossed strings, or turn the string back on itself before finishing with two half-hitches around its own standing part, as shown bottom right.

For greater security, you can make a Marling hitch (see page 29) or a half-hitch where the strings cross on the back of the parcel.

A Christmas parcel or other fancy package is usually tied with a *Bow*. To do this pass the middle of the string behind the parcel, and bring the ends to the front. Pass with a half-hitch and go round again at right-angles to the first binding. At the other side,

take one end round the first binding in a half-hitch before bringing the two ends together for the Bow. Tie them together as in the first half of a Reef Knot. Then complete a Reef Knot with two loops instead of two ends. This Bow could also be referred to as a *Double Slip Reef Knot*. Shoes are tied with the same Bow, of course.

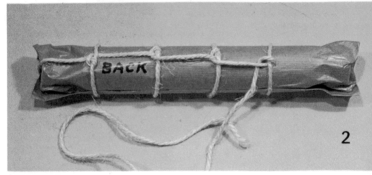

A very long parcel can be dealt with as follows: make a running noose around one end and hold it with a couple of half-hitches. Take the string along the parcel a little way and take a turn round the parcel itself. Pass the end of the string under the turn you have just made and make a half-hitch.

Then proceed down the parcel by what a sailor would call *Marling* (you can see how this is done in the first picture above). Hold each section taut with one hand as you make the next hitch with the other.

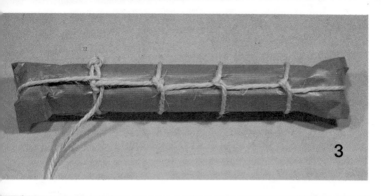

3

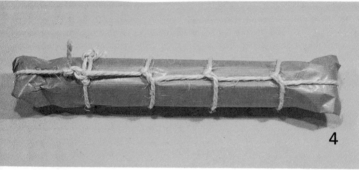

4

Arriving at the other end, take your string from the last Marling Hitch round the end of the parcel and back on the other side, half-hitching round each Marling loop as you go. Finally hitch round your starting knot, and grip with two or three half-hitches on top of one another as before.

These methods of tying parcels can be adapted for other shapes of bundle. The running noose enables you to pull the bundle very tight, but don't over-estimate the strength of your string! You can get such a strong pull by this method that you may snap it.

Hitches

We have referred already to a hitch, or a half-hitch. A hitch is a method of attaching a rope to another rope (or other object) without using a full knot, but making use of the tension on the rope, the direction of pull, or the influence of nearby knots to hold the hitch in place.

Hitches are very useful only when, through experience,

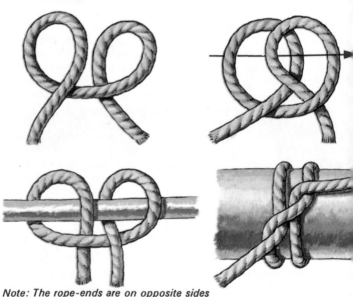

Note: The rope-ends are on opposite sides of the horizontal rod

you understand how each is to be used, and what its weaknesses are.

The best-known hitch is the *Clove Hitch* which is often tied by taking two loops and slipping a rod through them in the direction shown by the arrow. Often however this hitch needs to be made on a mast or post where the loops cannot be slipped on from the end.

In that case the Clove Hitch is made like this: take the rope from your right round the post, and back under the standing part of the rope. Then take the second turn around the post above the first and *in the same direction* (you feel that it should go in the opposite direction!) Then finish by bringing the end out *under* the second turn, as shown in the picture.

This hitch will take an outwards or a downwards strain without slipping.

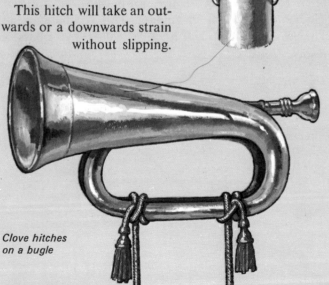

Clove hitches on a bugle

Another simple hitch is the *Timber Hitch*, so called because it is useful for lifting or dragging a log, or similar object. It is simply made by taking a rope end round the timber; hitching it round its own standing part and back to tuck under itself round and round several times. This can be done with the standing part of the rope already taut.

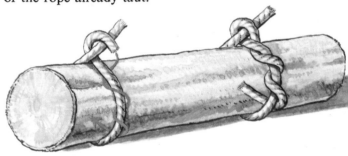

If the log is going to be dragged sideways, a half-hitch round the log further down helps to stop the Timber Hitch from unwinding. This combination of Timber Hitch and half-hitch is called by sailors a *Killick Hitch*.

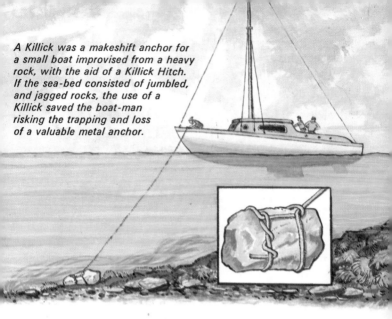

A Killick was a makeshift anchor for a small boat improvised from a heavy rock, with the aid of a Killick Hitch. If the sea-bed consisted of jumbled, and jagged rocks, the use of a Killick saved the boat-man risking the trapping and loss of a valuable metal anchor.

A hitch which looks alarmingly unsafe, but is sometimes used where a quick release may be needed, is the *Slippery Hitch*. In this the end of a rope is taken round a pin or cleat, and a bight is merely tucked under its own standing part as shown. It will only hold if the standing part of the rope draws down on the tucked bight with a steady strain.

Here is a hitch which you may like to try for fun. It is called the *Highwayman's Hitch*, but does equally well for cowboys, or the family pet! Bring up a loop from near the end of the tethering-rope behind the hitching-post, as in the picture. Then gather a second loop from the standing part of the rope, and bring it up in front of the hitching rail to tuck it through the first loop,

pulling the first loop tighter to hold it in position.
Finally gather the end of the rope into yet another loop,
which is brought in front of the rail and tucked through
the second loop which is tightened down by heaving
on the standing part of the rope. No matter how hard
the tethered animal pulls, the hitch will not come
undone, and yet a sharp tug on the hanging rope end
will release it straightaway (as you leap into the saddle!)

In the same situation of hitching up to a rail, the small-boat sailor would use a *Round Turn and Two Half-Hitches*. This knot is very easy to make, and it will stand any amount of joggling about while remaining easy to undo when no longer needed.

To make it you merely take a 'round turn' with the rope-end around a convenient rail or ring. Then take a half-hitch around the standing part of the rope, as in the picture, and a second half-hitch above the first. Waggoners and lorrydrivers sometimes use the same knot with the second half-hitch made with a bight, when they are tying down their loads.

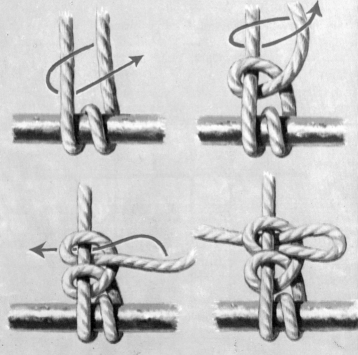

We described the Fisherman's Knot on page 18. There is a *Fisherman's Bend* which is a variant of the Round Turn and Two Half-Hitches in which the rope is taken under the Round Turn in making the first half-hitch. The second half-hitch is made in the usual way.

Old-time sailors used quite a collection of bends of this type, each of which was particularly suitable for a specific task on a sailing ship. Their names often indicate their purpose, as in the *Tops'l Halyard Bend*. They generally start with one or two turns around the spar to which a rope is to be attached.

Sheet Bend

We mentioned in connection with the Reef Knot its main weakness – that it is not suitable for joining ropes whose thicknesses are greatly different. A Reef Knot used under such conditions would slip dangerously, and this is a clear case for the *Sheet Bend*.

To make this bend the end of the larger rope is doubled back, and the end of the smaller rope is pushed through the resulting loop from behind. Emerging at the front, it is taken round the back of the bight from left to right, and back to the front. Here it is tucked under its own rope where it comes out of the heavier bight.

This knot will only take a pull on the end (*a*). If the other thin end is pulled, the bend comes undone. Additional security can be obtained if you take an extra turn around the large bight before tucking in, thereby making a *Double Sheet Bend*.

Note: Working ends marked in red

Bowline Bend

The single and double Sheet Bend are also useful for attaching fishing-line to the loop of a gut or nylon cast.

This knot is also called the *Weaver's Knot*, because it is used by a weaver to join his threads. He has a different method of making the knot, but the result is the same. The Weaver's Knot is also used in net-making.

The other advantage of the Sheet Bend is that it does not slip, even when joining two wet ropes, or ropes of very different thickness. A sailor, however, would probably make two interlinked Bowlines (a *Bowline Bend*) in such cases.

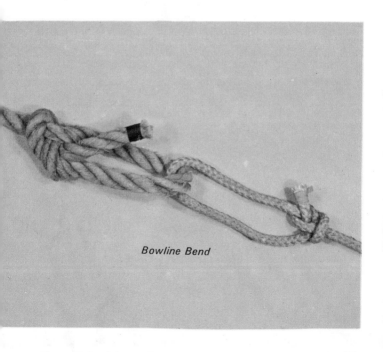

Bowline Bend

Sheepshank

One other task you may have to perform on a rope is to shorten it while the ends are in use. The knot for this job is the *Sheepshank*, best tied as follows: lay the rope across your hand in an elongated 'S' shape and take a half-hitch around each bight of the 'S' with the straight rope alongside. There is another method of tying this knot, starting from three half-hitches, but this method is no quicker, and gives an untidy twist to the finished knot.

However there is an interesting and quickly-tied variant of the Sheepshank. Make a slip loop and pull the loop through as far as you need to tighten the rope. Then simply hold the loop with a half-hitch on the nearby standing part of the rope (on *either* side). This knot is easily undone by loosening the half-hitch, and tugging at the ends of the slip knot.

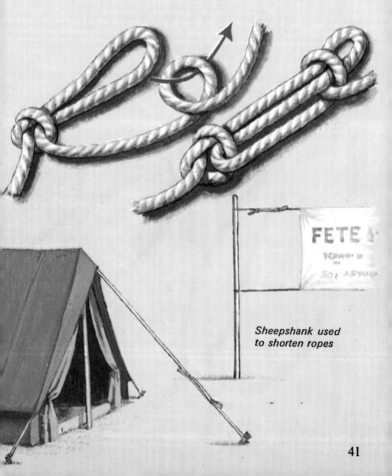

Sheepshank used to shorten ropes

Simple Sennit

Some methods of shortening ropes are attractive to look at, and can be used for decorative purposes. Most people know how to plait three ropes together (or three bunches of hair), but it is possible to achieve the same effect with a single rope. Lay the rope back on itself in a long loop, as in the picture. Then bring the left-hand section of the rope 'a' to the middle by twisting the loop over to the left. Bring the loose end of rope 'b' round,

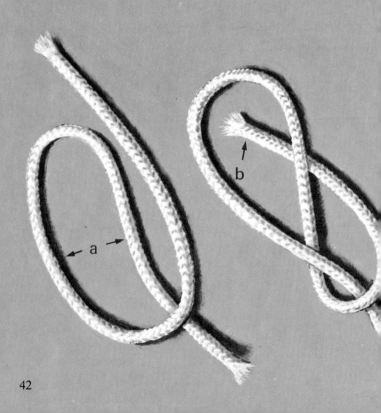

through the loop from the back, and across to the left. Next twist the loop again to bring the new right-hand section through to the middle, and cross end 'a' to the right, coming through the loop from the back again. Continue bringing outside-to-middle as in ordinary plaiting, by twisting the loop first one way, then the other, as necessary. Finish by taking the end through the far end of the loop, and tightening, and evening-up the chain. Sailors called this the *Simple Sennit* or *Plait Knot*.

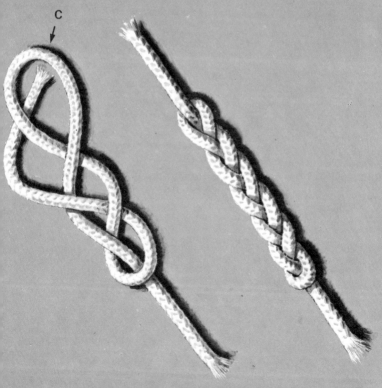

Chain knots

A *Single Chain Knot* is made by starting with a slip knot, then gathering a bight from the rest of the rope and passing it through the loop of the Slip Knot, which is then pulled tight. Gather a new bight, and pass it through the loop of the last bight, and continue doing this again and again, for as long as you like. Fasten the resulting Chain Knot by passing the end through the last loop. This chain is easily undone by pulling the end from the last loop, and giving the rope-ends a sharp tug, which will make all of the loops pull out in turn.

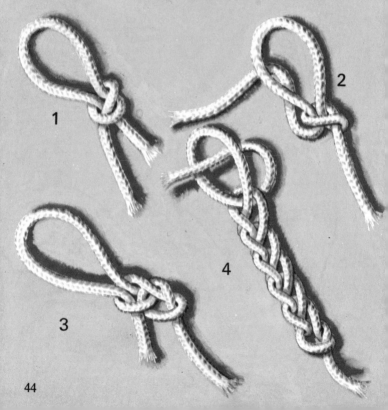

Take care when making the chain that your rope-end is always on the same side as you make the loops, otherwise you will make an ugly twist. Also, for speed, don't let the loops get too big. And talking of speed: this is the *Drummer's Chain Knot* which features in the *Guinness Book of Records* in a knotting speed record, and is shown in the drum drag-ropes below.

Simple whipping

Simple whipping is easy to master, and can even be done on fine cord with strong sewing cotton, if your fingers are nimble.

When whipping rope, it is best to cover a length two or three times as great as the thickness of your rope with the turns of fine twine. To begin whipping you double back the end of your whipping-cord to form a loop (or bight) and lay this along the end of your rope with the loop sticking out slightly beyond the rope's end, with the short end of your whipping-cord pointing back to the main part of your rope as in the picture.

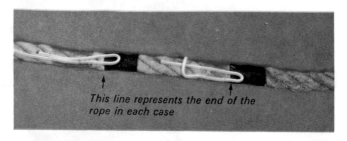

This line represents the end of the rope in each case

Next, you take the rest of the cord (which need not be detached from its reel or skein) and begin to wind it round the rope's end, with the first turn crossing over the short end of your loop before going round the back of the rope. This first turn should be about three rope widths away from the end of the rope, and the later turns must be made tightly, evenly, and as close together as possible. Work round and round towards the end of the rope, and against the twist of the rope, as in these pictures.

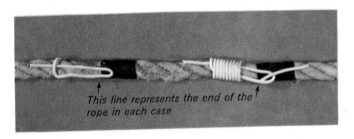

This line represents the end of the rope in each case

When you have almost reached the end of the rope with your whipping, cut away a centimetre or two more of cord from the reel (if still attached) and push the end through the loop which you made at the beginning. Then, holding this last turn so that it doesn't escape, pull the short end of your original loop so that the loop draws back under the whipping, pulling the last turn of whipping with it. This will stop the whipping from coming undone. Trim off the spare ends of cord close to your whipping to leave it neat.

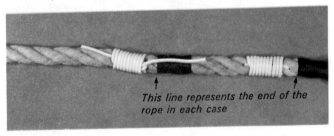

This line represents the end of the rope in each case

To make this whipping as secure as possible, make the whipping turns tight and close and don't go too close to the end of the rope. When whipping with thread on a slippery nylon cord, you can give the whipping a thin layer of nail varnish or polyurethane varnish for extra security.

47

Whipping knots

Whipping turns are also used in making two of the knots used in tying nylon fishing line onto a metal hook. The problem here is that the hook would tend to chafe the line until it broke if a single-loop knot were used. It is therefore essential for the knot to take the strain on as many turns of line as possible.

One suitable knot is the Whipping or *Domhof Knot*. In this knot you take the end of the line down through the eye of the hook and double back an end about twice as long as the hook. Using this end, make whipping turns round the shank of the hook and the double thickness of line from the eye of the hook downwards as far as necessary. Tuck the end of the last turn through the loop as in simple whipping, and lock it and tighten up the knot by hauling back the line through the eye of the hook. The downward strain of the hook is borne by the whipping turns together, and any chafing at the top should be spotted by the observant angler before there is any danger of losing the hook.

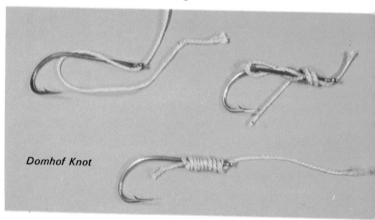

Domhof Knot

The disadvantage of this method of tying-on is that the knot is rather bulky for finer hooks. An alternative is the *Double Cairnton Knot*, shown below.

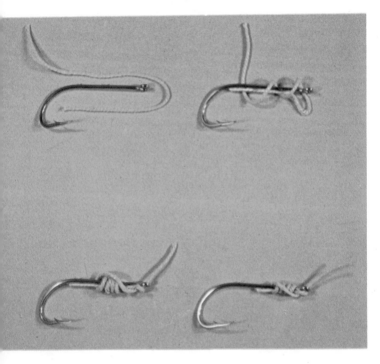

In this the end of a piece of line is laid against the shank of the hook as in the picture. This is turned back at the eye of the hook to make a couple of whipping turns around the shank and the line-end. Finally the remainder of the line is turned back and tucked first through the bight of the line, and then through the eye of the hook, before pulling up. Once again, the strain is borne by the whipping turns.

Matthew Walker's knot

One whole family of knots which we have not yet dealt with in this book is that group which is made by separating the strands of a rope, then tying or weaving them back together. Knots of this type can be purely decorative or they can make a useful stopper or knob on a rope. Splices for joining ropes or making 'Eyes' in ropes are begun in the same way of course, but in this book we leave you with one final knot as a challenge.

It is called the *Matthew Walker*, or in the old days, *Matthew Walker's Knot*. Strictly speaking this is the doubled form of the knot, which is more satisfying to make. It is believed to have been described, if not named, in a seamen's dictionary of the seventeenth century.

Begin by parting the strands of the rope for a distance of about 15 cm from the end. At your first attempt, mark the ends of the strands with different colours of felt-tip pen. Also tie a thin piece of string round the rope just below where you intend to start the knot, to stop any unravelling as you work. (At the end this is cut off and discarded.) Take one of the strands and lead it loosely round the rope and up through its own bight when you reach it (1). Take the next strand round below the first and up through its bight, before bringing the second strand up through its own bight (2). Take the last strand round below the others, and up through their bights, before bringing it up through its own bight (3).

Finally, holding the knot down between two fingers, tighten up the strands in rotation, until the knot is tight and neat. It should look like No. 4 in the picture. If the strands do not lie parallel, ease them into position with a fingertip.

This knot was a favourite for holding the rope handles into a seaman's chest, and for decorated ropes. Seamen are supposed to have puzzled landlubbers by unravelling a rope to its middle, tying a Matthew Walker there, and twisting the strands back together again. They then challenged some unlucky person to undo the knot! YOU know the secret!

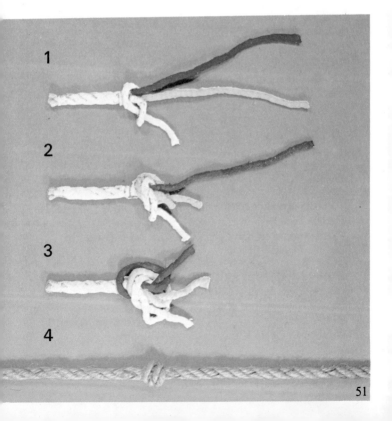

INDEX